ENVY

A DICTIONARY FOR THE JEALOUS

Aadamsmedia
Avon, Massachusetts

Published by
Adams Media, a division of F+W Media, Inc.
57 Littlefield Street, Avon, MA 02322. U.S.A.
www.adamsmedia.com

ISBN 10: 1-4405-2802-0
ISBN 13: 978-1-4405-2802-6
eISBN 10: 1-4405-2827-6
eISBN 13: 978-1-4405-2827-9

Printed in the United States of America.

10   9   8   7   6   5   4   3   2   1

Library of Congress Cataloging-in-Publication Data
is available from the publisher.

This publication is designed to provide accurate and authoritative information with regard to the subject matter covered. It is sold with the understanding that the publisher is not engaged in rendering legal, accounting, or other professional advice. If legal advice or other expert assistance is required, the services of a competent professional person should be sought.

 —From a *Declaration of Principles* jointly adopted by a Committee of the American Bar Association and a Committee of Publishers and Associations

Many of the designations used by manufacturers and sellers to distinguish their product are claimed as trademarks. Where those designations appear in this book and Adams Media was aware of a trademark claim, the designations have been printed with initial capital letters.

Interior illustration © clipart.com.

This book is available at quantity discounts for bulk purchases.
For information, please call 1-800-289-0963.

An Introduction to
Envy

envy

(EN-vee)

NOUN: The desire to have the possessions or status
of another.

Everyone wants what someone else has—whether or
not anyone wants to admit to it is an entirely differ-
ent story. However, throughout literature there have
been many tales of the turmoil and treachery that
this desirous want has caused. From the deceitful
Iago in Shakespeare's *Othello* to the wicked queens
in many a fairy tale to Baron Danglars in Dumas'
The Count of Monte Cristo, all are testaments to the
power of the pains the green-eyed monster creates.
While envy is defined best in a wanting gaze, this
desirable dictionary captures the spirit of the most
covetous sin.

A

abhor
(*ab-HAWR*)
VERB: To regard with aversion and disgust.

abhorrent
(*ab-HAWR-uhnt*)
ADJECTIVE: Causing disgust and repugnance.

> *Clara's thoughts toward Benjamin's newly announced fiancée were ABHORRENT and completely against how she was raised, yet she could not help herself as he walked her out in front of the crowd at their engagement dinner.*

abominable
(*uh-BOM-uh-nuh-buhl*)
ADJECTIVE: Hateful or detestable.

accomplish
(*uh-KOM-plish*)
VERB: To successfully complete, as in a task.

accomplishments
(*uh-KOM-plish-muhnts*)
NOUN: Achievements; a successfully completed task; ability or skill.

acerbate
(*AS-er-bayt*)
VERB: To embitter.

acerbic
(*uh-SUR-bik*)
ADJECTIVE: Sharp or harsh language; sour language.

ache for
(*ayk for*)
VERB: A strong desire for something or someone.

acidity
(*uh-SID-ih-tee*)
NOUN: The measure of bite or sharpness in one's tone.

acidulous
(*uh-SIDJ-uh-luss*)
ADJECTIVE: A way of speaking that sounds bitter or sharp.

adulation
(*ad-yoo-LAY-shun*)
NOUN: Extreme praise, admiration, or flattery, especially of a servile nature. *Adulation* generally implies acclaim and admiration that is out of scope with its object.

From envy, hatred,

and malice, and all

uncharitableness,

Good Lord, deliver us.

—BOOK OF COMMON PRAYER

advantage

(*ad-VAN-tijz*)

NOUN: Beneficial position in a circumstance; opportunity others might not have; often used in plural.

> *It is not so much the material possessions her more privileged classmates enjoy but instead the ADVANTAGE their social standing gives them after they matriculate that Isabelle wishes she also had.*

advantaged

(*ad-VAN-tijd*)

ADJECTIVE: The state of having a beneficial or favorable position.

adversary

(*AD-ver-sar-ee*)

NOUN: An opponent, enemy, or foe.

aesthetic

(*us-THET-ik*)

ADJECTIVE: Of or related to a sense of what is attractive or beautiful. Also: Related to sensation and feeling as contrasted with reason or logic. *Aesthetics* is the science that examines how people react to art and beauty. Something that is aesthetically pleasing is in keeping with one's standards of scale, structure, clarity, and attractiveness.

affinity

(*uh-FIN-ih-tee*)

NOUN: A natural liking or affection.

aggravate

(*AG-ruh-vayt*)

VERB: To annoy. Also, make worse.

aggravation

(*ag-ruh-VAY-shuhn*)

NOUN: The state of being aggravated.

> *The bride's eldest sister felt such strong AGGRAVATION over not being chosen as the maid of honor that she thought it best not to attend the ceremony at all.*

agonize

(*AG-uh-nyz*)

VERB: To suffer pain.

agony

(*AG-uh-nee*)

NOUN: The state of intense pain and suffering.

alieni appetens

(*AY-lee-EN-ee AP-uh-tens*)

NOUN: A Latin term meaning to covet another person's possessions.

allege
(*uh-LEDJ*)
VERB: To accuse someone of something—usually wrongdoing—without proof.

allegiance
(*uh-LEE-junce*)
NOUN: Extreme loyalty.

allure
(*uh-LOOR*)
NOUN: The quality of being tempting, seductive.

alluring
(*uh-LOO-ring*)
ADJECTIVE: Tempting; seductive.

ambitious
(*am-BISH-uhs*)
ADJECTIVE: Strongly determined; desirous to succeed.

amoral

(*ay-MOR-uhl*)

ADJECTIVE: Without moral discretion or standards; without standards of right and wrong. To be amoral is to act as though the distinctions of right and wrong are nonexistent. A person who is *amoral* is neither moral nor immoral.

amoralism

(*ay-MOR-uhl-izm*)

NOUN: The state of acting without moral discretion or standards.

anger

(*ANG-er*)

NOUN: A feeling of hostility or intense displeasure.

John's jealousy quickly turned to ANGER when he realized that not only was his archrival being promoted over him but that he was being demoted as well.

angry

(*ANG-ree*)

ADJECTIVE: Feeling or showing anger.

animosity

(*an-uh-MOS-ih-tee*)

NOUN: A feeling of hostility or strong dislike.

Base envy withers

at another's joy.

—JAMES THOMSON

animus
(*AN-uh-muhs*)
NOUN: Ill will; hostility; dislike.

antagonist
(*an-TAG-uh-nist*)
NOUN: An opponent or adversary. In a story, the one working against the main character.

antipathy
(*an-TIP-uh-thee*)
NOUN: Aversion; strong dislike.

ape
(*ayp*)
VERB: Imitate or mimic a person's behavior.

appetence
(*AP-eh-tents*)
NOUN: Intense longing or desire; a natural craving.

> *Mr. Thorndike's APPETENCE for an aged scotch makes him envy those who can afford decadent dinners and cocktails every night.*

Argus-eyed

(*AHR-guhs-ahyd*)

ADJECTIVE: Vigilantly observant. In Greek mythology, Argos is said to have had one hundred eyes, and Hera ordered him to keep watch on all those that she was jealous of.

arrogate

(*AYR-uh-gayt*)

VERB: To demand something for oneself or to take control without authority.

askance

(*uh-SKANS*)

ADVERB: With a look of disapproval or mistrust.

asperity

(*a-SPAYR-ih-tee*)

NOUN: Carrying with it a multitude of meanings, *asperity* most often refers to a harshness of manner. It also means "hard to endure."

aspersion

(*uh-SPUR-zhun*)

NOUN: False accusation; slander. To *cast an aspersion* on another is to make an unfair or untrue statement about his or her conduct or character.

aspiration

(*ass-puh-RAY-shun*)

NOUN: Goal; desire; something one wishes to achieve.

> *Marco, whose lifelong ASPIRATION was to be the number one seat violinist in the orchestra, was left thinking only about sabotage when it was announced the young prodigy would be assuming the premiere position.*

aspire

(*uhs-PYR*)

VERB: To hope to achieve something; eagerly desirous.

athirst

(*uh-THERST*)

ADJECTIVE: Thirsty or eager for something.

B

backbiter
(*BAK-byt-er*)
NOUN: A person who speaks negatively or maliciously about someone who is not present.

backbiting
(*BAK-byt-ing*)
ADJECTIVE: Negative or malicious in nature, usually about someone who is not present.

bad blood
(*bad bluhd*)
NOUN: Animosity; unfriendly relations between two or more parties, usually spawned from a previous conflict.

badly
(*BAD-lee*)
ADVERB: Very much; severely.

bank
(*bangk*)
NOUN: An establishment where monetary transactions take place and currency is safeguarded; also personal wealth, informally.

Envy consists in seeing

things never in themselves,

but only in their relations.

If you desire glory, you may

envy Napoleon,

but Napoleon envied Caesar,

Caesar envied Alexander,

and Alexander, I daresay,

envied Hercules,

who never existed.

—BERTRAND RUSSELL

beauty

(*BYOO-tee*)

NOUN: The quality possessed by a person or thing that causes deep satisfaction and fascination.

beg

(*beg*)

VERB: To plead for charity.

beget

(*bih-GET*)

VERB: To cause.

begrudge

(*bee-GRUDGE*)

VERB: To give or grant reluctantly.

bitter

(*BIT-er*)

ADJECTIVE: Resentful or hurt due to a sense of unfair treatment.

> *The BITTER taste of covetous desire put a quick end to the long friendship the two young men shared once the one woman they both pursued chose one over the other.*

bitterness

(*BIT-er-nuhs*)

NOUN: A sense of resentment or hurt due to a feeling of having been treated unfairly.

blackmail

(*BLAK-mayl*)

VERB: To extort money from a person by threatening to expose a secret.

brooding

(*BROO-ding*)

ADJECTIVE: Preoccupied with unhappiness of thought or painful memories.

> *One look at Thomas's BROODING eyes and Delilah knew he was thinking back to yesterday's game, when his rival clobbered him on the field.*

brook no rival

(*bruhk no RY-vuhl*)

VERB: Not tolerate anyone to beat oneself.

burn for

(*buhrn for*)

VERB: To want or desire something intensely.

C

Cain

(*kayn*)

NOUN: The character in the Bible who murders his brother because of his own jealousy.

> *Jeffery chose to downplay his own successes whenever talking in front of his brother, since Mark was truly the CAIN to Jeffrey's Abel and such conversations only created controversy.*

calumniate

(*kuh-LUHM-nee-ayt*)

VERB: To make malicious, false, defamatory statements about someone.

calumniator

(*kuh-LUHM-nee-ayt-or*)

NOUN: A person who makes malicious, false statements about someone else.

calumnious

(*kuh-LUHM-nee-uhs*)

ADJECTIVE: Full of malice towards someone; slandering someone's reputation.

calumny

(*kuh-LUHM-nee*)

NOUN: Malicious, false statements about someone.

caustic
(*KOSS-tik*)
ADJECTIVE: Corrosive or capable of burning. Something is *caustic* if it can eat away at something else. A person is *caustic* if he speaks sharply and maliciously.

chagrin
(*shuh-GRIN*)
NOUN: A feeling of embarrassment or humiliation.

challenge
(*CHAL-inj*)
NOUN: A competition.

challenger
(*CHAL-lin-jer*)
NOUN: A person who is apt to challenge others to a competition; person who vies for the position of an incumbent.

choose
(*chooz*)
VERB: To pick or select; to want.

churlish
(*CHUR-lish*)
ADJECTIVE: Ill-bred; boorish.

combatant

(*kuhm-BAT-nt*)

NOUN: A group or person engaged in a fight.

competition

(*kom-pi-TI-shuhn*)

NOUN: An event where people compete against each other or themselves; a contest.

competitive

(*kuhm-PET-ih-tiv*)

ADJECTIVE: Characterized by competition.

competitiveness

(*kuhm-PET-ih-tiv-ness*)

NOUN: The state or degree of being competitive.

concentrate

(*KON-sen-trayt*)

VERB: To focus attention.

conflict

(*KAHN-flikt*)

NOUN: A disagreement or issue between people or groups.

> *When it comes to properly resolving a CONFLICT, it is important that both parties are amenable to the final terms.*

consumed

(*kuhn-SOOMD*)

VERB: To be used up or ingested, as in *consumed with*.

contempt

(*kuhn-TEMPT*)

NOUN: Disdain; the thought or feeling that something or someone is deserving of scorn; the state of being disdained.

contemptible

(*kuhn-TEMPT-ih-buhl*)

ADJECTIVE: Deserving of scorn or contempt.

contemptuous

(*kuhn-TEMP-choo-us*)

ADJECTIVE: Showing scorn or contempt.

contend

(*kuhn-TEND*)

VERB: To compete with.

contender

(*kuhn-TEND-er*)

NOUN: One who contends; one who has a good chance of victory.

Envy is the art of counting

the other fellow's blessings

instead of your own.

—HAROLD COFFIN

contest

(*KAHN-test*)

NOUN: A competition between two or more people.

copy

(*KAH-pee*)

NOUN: A replica of something.

VERB: To make a replica or similar version of something; to imitate another's actions.

copycat

(*KAH-pee-kat*)

NOUN: A person who mimics another's behavior or ideas.

> *It is sad to watch Richard act like such a COPYCAT, simply following suit with whatever William has seen success with in the past, since he does not feel he can keep up with his competitor.*

corrupt

(*kuh-RUHPT*)

ADJECTIVE: Dishonest action, usually in pursuit of money or other forms of personal gain.

corruption

(*kuh-RUHP-shun*)

NOUN: Conduct that is dishonest in action, usually motivated by money or other form of gain.

cotton to
(*KAH-ten to*)
VERB: To have a liking for.

covet
(*KUHV-it*)
VERB: To yearn for or desire.

> *The Bible repeatedly warns against the dangers of COVETING your neighbor's possessions and even goes so far to call out such sinful desires in the Ten Commandments.*

covetous
(*KUHV-ih-tuss*)
ADJECTIVE: Greedy and willing to go to shameless lengths to earn wealth.

covetousness
(*KUHV-ih-tuss-ness*)
NOUN: The act of being greedy and shameless.

crave
(*krayv*)
VERB: To strongly desire or yearn for.

craver
(*KRAY-ver*)
NOUN: A person who longs or desires.

craving
(*KRAY-ving*)
NOUN: An intense desire or yearning.

cupidinous
(*kyoo-PID-in-us*)
ADJECTIVE: Denoting greed.

cupidity
(*kyoo-PID-ih-tee*)
NOUN: Greed; extreme desire for wealth. One who is obsessed with acquiring money shows *cupidity*.

cynical
(*SIN-ih-kuhl*)
ADJECTIVE: Distrusting and doubtful in a bitter, pessimistic way.

D

defamatory

(*dih-FAHM-uh-tor-ee*)

ADJECTIVE: To speak or write in a manner that attacks someone's reputation.

defame

(*dih-FAYM*)

VERB: To attack or damage the reputation of another person.

defensive

(*dih-FEN-siv*)

ADJECTIVE: Concerned with guarding one's reputation.

depravity

(*dih-PRAV-ih-tee*)

NOUN: Corruption; moral reprehensibility. Someone who corrupts something or introduces wickedness to it demonstrates *depravity*.

deserve

(*dih-ZURV*)

VERB: To be worthy of or qualified for something.

deserving

(*dih-ZUR-ving*)

ADJECTIVE: Worthy.

desiderate

(*dih-SID-uh-rayt*)

VERB: To desire or wish for.

desideratum

(*dih-sid-uh-RAH-tum*)

NOUN: A thing to be desired. *Desideratum* finds its plural in *desiderata,* which is also the name of a popular short writing that outlines worthy spiritual objectives.

> *He eventually accepted that her love was a fleeting DESIDERATUM, one he could learn in time to do without.*

desirable

(*dih-ZAHY-rah-buhl*)

ADJECTIVE: The state of being wanted.

desire

(*dih-ZYR*)

VERB: To want or crave.

NOUN: Longing or feeling of wanting.

desirous

(*dih-ZY-russ*)

ADJECTIVE: Characterized by desire.

detestable

(*dih-TESS-tih-buhl*)

ADJECTIVE: Deserving of hatred or dislike.

detract

(*dih-TRAKT*)

VERB: Reduce or take away from.

detraction

(*dih-TRAKT-shuhn*)

NOUN: The act of detracting or taking away; something or someone who detracts or takes away from.

detractive

(*dih-TRAK-tiv*)

ADJECTIVE: Having the quality of taking away.

detractor

(*dih-TRAKT-or*)

NOUN: One who disparages others.

> *While Daniel was surrounded by a number of suitors, Samantha took it as an opportunity to be his biggest DETRACTOR, hoping to drive them away in an effort to win his attention for herself.*

You can't be envious and

happy at the same time.

—Frank Tyger

devour

(*dih-VOWR*)

VERB: To eat or consume quickly, voraciously, and entirely.

die

(*dahy*)

VERB: As in *to die for*; an informal way of saying that one is extremely desirous of something or someone.

disaffect

(*dis-uh-FEKT*)

VERB: To alienate or become disloyal.

disaffection

(*dis-uh-FECK-shuhn*)

NOUN: Being dissatisfied with people in authority.

With two groups vying to take control of the majority vote, the board of directors called a meeting to discuss the growing DISAFFECTION among the members.

disapprobation

(*dis-ap-ruh-BAY-shuhn*)

NOUN: Disapproval, sometimes social.

disconcerting

(*diss-kun-SERT-ing*)

ADJECTIVE: Upsetting; disturbing to harmony or balance.

discontent

(*dis-kun-TENT*)

NOUN: The state of not being happy; dissatisfaction.

discontented

(*dis-kun-TENT-ed*)

ADJECTIVE: Unhappy with one's circumstances.

discontentment

(*dis-kun-TENT-ment*)

NOUN: A state of being unhappy or unsatisfied.

discourteous

(*dis-KER-tee-us*)

ADJECTIVE: Showing rudeness.

discredit

(*dis-KRED-it*)

VERB: To damage or harm the reputation of someone or something.

discriminatory

(*dis-KRIM-in-ah-tor-ee*)
ADJECTIVE: Showing prejudice; biased.

disgruntled

(*dis-GRUN-tulld*)
ADJECTIVE: Angry; dissatisfied.

disgruntlement

(*dis-GRUN-tull-ment*)
NOUN: The state of being disgruntled.

disillusion

(*dis-il-LOO-zhuhn*)
NOUN: The feeling resulting from being freed from
false beliefs or understandings.
VERB: To free from illusion; to disenchant.

disparage

(*dis-PAR-ij*)
VERB: To belittle or represent as not having value or
worth.

> *The aging tennis champion took any opportunity
> he was presented to DISPARAGE his younger
> competition, no matter how quickly they were gaining
> on him in terms of tournaments won.*

displeasure

(*dis-PLEH-zhur*)

NOUN: A feeling of unhappy annoyance.

dissatisfaction

(*dis-sat-is-FAK-shuhn*)

NOUN: A state of displeasure.

dissatisfied

(*dis-SAT-is-fyed*)

ADJECTIVE: Unhappy or displeased.

distraught

(*dih-STRAWT*)

ADJECTIVE: Deeply hurt emotionally.

distrust

(*dis-TRUHST*)

NOUN: A lack of trust; a feeling of skepticism.

VERB: The act of not trusting.

distrustful

(*dis-TRUHST-ful*)

ADJECTIVE: Full of doubt; not able to trust.

ditto

(*DIT-oh*)

NOUN: The same as someone else said; a duplicate.

doubt

(*dowt*)

NOUN: A feeling of uncertainty.

VERB: To be uncertain of.

> *After she discovered the truth about her husband's infidelity, Katherine began to DOUBT whether he was ever really attracted to her.*

dream

(*dreem*)

NOUN: An aspiration; something that is longed for.

VERB: To imagine.

drool

(*drool*)

VERB: To salivate; to show eagerness for pleasure.

dudgeon

(*DUH-juhn*)

NOUN: A feeling of resentment and anger.

dysphoria

(*dys-FOR-ee-uh*)

NOUN: Dissatisfaction with life.

When men are full of envy

they disparage everything,

whether it be good or bad.

—TACITUS

E

eager
(*EE-ger*)
ADJECTIVE: Keen desire; wanting something very much.

eagerness
(*EE-ger-ness*)
NOUN: The state of being eager.

eaten up
(*EET-n uhp*)
ADJECTIVE: Completely consumed.

echo
(*EK-oh*)
VERB: To repeat.

embitter
(*em-BIT-er*)
VERB: To make bitter.

> *Years of wanting a promotion and not receiving it had EMBITTERED the middle-aged accountant.*

emulate
(*EM-yoo-layt*)
VERB: To imitate, usually in an attempt to better oneself; to use another's actions as a model for future success or mastery.

emulative

(*EM-yoo-la-tiv*)

ADJECTIVE: A way of acting or speaking that shows imitation.

emulous

(*EM-yoo-luss*)

VERB: To seek to emulate.

emulousness

(*EM-yoo-luss-ness*)

NOUN: The quality of being emulous.

enemy

(*EN-em-ee*)

NOUN: A hostile opponent; one opposed to one's own well-being.

engross

(*en-GROHS*)

VERB: To completely absorb one's attention.

enjoy

(*en-JOI*)

VERB: Take delight; find pleasure in.

enmity
(*EN-mi-tee*)
NOUN: Ill will; hostility; hatred.

ennui
(*ahn-WEE*)
NOUN: Listlessness, dissatisfaction, or boredom.
Ennui is French for "boredom."

envenom
(*en-VEN-uhm*)
VERB: To embitter.

enviable
(*EN-vee-uh-buhl*)
ADJECTIVE: Arousing envy.

envier
(*EN-vee-er*)
NOUN: One who envies.

envious
(*EN-vee-us*)
ADJECTIVE: Showing envy.

envy

(*EN-vee*)

NOUN: The desire to have the possessions or status of another.

VERB: To strongly desire something belonging to someone else.

> *Sometimes it is not ENVYING material goods that is most painful, but instead it is the desire to be as happy as those around you that causes the most grief.*

-envy

(*EN-vee*)

SUFFIX: Denotes something one might be jealous or envious of, as in *career-envy, house-envy, pet-envy*.

equal

(*EE-kwil*)

ADJECTIVE: Having the same size or degree.

NOUN: One who is the same status as another.

eternal triangle

(*ih-TUR-nl TRAHY-ang-guhl*)

NOUN: A rivalry between three people, usually involving a couple and an additional lover. Also referred to as a love triangle.

Do not overrate what you

have received, nor envy

others. He who envies

others does not obtain

peace of mind.

—Buddha

evil eye
(*EE-vuhl ahy*)
NOUN: A wicked look that is thought to inflict misfortune on the person it is directed toward.

eyes for
(*ahyz for*)
NOUN: To want a person or thing.

exaggerate
(*ig-ZAJ-uh-rayt*)
VERB: To inflate the truth.

> *Olive was known to EXAGGERATE her success in order to put herself on the same level as her peers.*

exasperate
(*ig-ZAS-puh-rayt*)
VERB: To annoy intensely.

expiate
(*EK-spee-ayt*)
VERB: Atone for sins.

F

facsimile
(*fak-SIM-uh-lee*)
NOUN: An exact copy, imitation, or reproduction.

fair
(*fayr*)
ADJECTIVE: Just or legitimate.

fairness
(*FAYR-nes*)
NOUN: The state of being fair.

faithful
(*FAYTH-ful*)
ADJECTIVE: Loyal; true.

faithfulness
(*FAYTH-ful-ness*)
NOUN: Loyalty; the state of being faithful.

fall for
(*fall for*)
VERB: To become infatuated with.

fancy

(*FAN-see*)

VERB: To desire, want, or like.

Victor really FANCIED his brother's girlfriend and spent as much time as he could trying to win her away.

fascinate

(*FAS-uh-nayt*)

VERB: To cause attention to be held or arouse interest.

fault

(*falt*)

NOUN: Unattractive or harmful quality.

fear

(*feer*)

NOUN: The thought that something unpleasant might happen.

VERB: To worry that something bad may happen, or already has.

fervor

(*FUR-ver*)

NOUN: Passionate feeling.

feud

(*fyood*)

NOUN: An unpleasant and sometimes hostile contention, usually lasting many years.

fidelity

(*fih-DEL-ih-tee*)

NOUN: Faithfulness; loyalty and support.

fixate

(*FIK-sate*)

VERB: To focus one's attention on, often to an alarming degree.

fixation

(*FIKS-ay-shuhn*)

NOUN: The state of being totally engrossed or preoccupied with someone or something.

focus

(*FOH-kus*)

VERB: To aim one's attention and concentration.

Tilly tried not to FOCUS on the fact that her best friend had just bought the necklace she had been eyeing for months.

Envy among other ingredients has a mixture of the love of justice in it. We are more angry at undeserved than at deserved good-fortune.

—WILLIAM HAZLITT

foe
(*FOH*)
NOUN: Enemy.

follow
(*FOL-oh*)
VERB: To take a page from someone else and do as he or she does.

fond
(*fond*)
ADJECTIVE: To have a great liking or inclination for.

fortune
(*FAWR-chuhn*)
NOUN: A vast wealth.

fret
(*freht*)
VERB: To worry.

fretter
(*FREHT-er*)
NOUN: One who is constantly anxious or worried.

Freud
(*froid*)
NOUN: A psychotherapist who enjoyed exploring the subconscious, especially as it related to envy and sex.

Freudian
(*FROI-dee-in*)
ADJECTIVE: Relating to the analysis of subconscious desires.
NOUN: Someone who follows Freud's doctrines.

Freudian slip
(*FROI-dee-in slip*)
NOUN: Saying something seemingly accidental that could hint at subconscious desires.

frustrate
(*FRUS-trayt*)
VERB: To upset or annoy, especially due to one's inability to achieve something.

frustration
(*FRUS-tray-shuhn*)
NOUN: A feeling of upset or annoyance.

> *Henry's FRUSTRATION over losing the match was compounded when he realized the winner would receive a kiss from Angela.*

G

gain
(*gayn*)
VERB: To obtain a thing one has desired.

gall
(*gawl*)
NOUN: Bitter effrontery.

gaſp for
(*gasp for*)
VERB: Crave; eagerly desire.

gatecrasher
(*GAYT-krash-er*)
NOUN: A person who attends a party or social function without invitation.

gaze
(*gayz*)
VERB: To ſtare longingly.

get
(*get*)
VERB: To obtain.

gimmes
(*GIM-ees*)
NOUN: Slang term standing for a state of wanting; short for "give me."

give eyeteeth for
(*giv AHY-teeth for*)
VERB: To give something of great value to one in order to gain something more desirable.

gloating
(*GLOHT-ing*)
NOUN: Dwelling on one's own success in a smug, malignant way.

glom onto
(*glahm on-tu*)
VERB: To look at with rapt attention; to steal or take possession of

gnawing
(*NAW-ing*)
NOUN: Persistent anxiety.

golden
(*GOHL-duhn*)
ADJECTIVE: Extremely valuable; prized.

Envy comes from people's

ignorance of, or lack of belief

in, their own gifts.

—JEAN VANIER

grab
(*grab*)
VERB: To grasþ or take something with force; to obtain quickly.

grabby
(*GRAB-bee*)
VERB: To take something with force due to desire.

grasþing
(*GRASP-ing*)
ADJECTIVE: Desiring the possessions of others, often through illegal or unethical means.

> *The GRASPING old man was caught sneaking into the homes of his wealthy neighbors.*

grasþingness
(*GRASP-ing-ness*)
NOUN: The quality of greedily desiring what others have.

gravitate
(*GRAV-ih-tayt*)
VERB: To have a natural inclination toward or be strongly attracted to.

greed
(*greed*)
NOUN: Excessive desire, often for wealth or power;
one of the seven deadly sins.

greedy
(*GREE-dee*)
ADJECTIVE: Having or showing greed; intense
wanting; selfish desire.

green
(*green*)
ADJECTIVE: Figuratively the color green, as with
envy or jealousy.

green-eyed monster
(*GREEN-ahyd MON-ster*)
NOUN: The personification of jealousy.

*Natasha watched for months in silence as her friend
openly flirted with the man she loved until finally the
GREEN-EYED MONSTER growing inside reared its
ugly head and she lashed out, screaming and yelling
and making a scene.*

grievances
(*GREE-vans-siz*)
NOUN: A feeling of being wronged.

Envy, like the worm, never

runs but to the fairest fruit;

like a cunning bloodhound,

it singles out the fattest deer

in the flock.

—FRANCIS BEAUMONT

grimace

(*GRIM-uss*)

NOUN: A facial contortion showing disgust or discomfort.

> *Billy GRIMACED every time Martin was referred to as his manager; he still could not believe he was passed up for the promotion and instead that fool's incompetence was rewarded.*

grudge

(*gruhj*)

NOUN: A feeling of ill will or resentment.

grudgingly

(*GRUHJ-ing-lee*)

ADVERB: To do something in a way that denotes ill will or resentment.

grumbler

(*GRUM-bler*)

NOUN: One who grumbles or voices discontent.

H

hanker

(*HAN-ker*)

VERB: Desire eagerly.

hankering

(*HAN-ker-ing*)

NOUN: A craving.

hate

(*hayt*)

VERB: Passionate feeling of dislike.

hate on

(*hayt on*)

VERB: To channel feelings of hate or jealousy onto someone or something.

The other children chose to HATE ON Phillip because his parents could afford him nice clothes to wear, which made him stand out in the group of urchinlike classmates.

hater

(*HAYT-er*)

NOUN: An alternate spelling of *hata*, slang for someone who is jealous.

Envy is an insult to oneself.

—Yevgeny Yevtushenko

haterade
(*HAYT-er-ayd*)
NOUN: A slang term meaning something that someone who is often jealous or negative is drinking.

hatred
(*HAY-tred*)
NOUN: Intense feelings of hate.

haunt
(*hawnt*)
VERB: To linger; to visit a place often.

have
(*hav*)
VERB: To possess.

> *Cliché or not, we always want what we cannot HAVE.*

have eyes for
(*hav ahyz for*)
NOUN: To like someone or something; be desirous of that person or thing.

have the hots for
(*hav the hots for*)
VERB: To desire someone in a sexual way.

heed
(*heed*)
VERB: To take someone's guidance; to listen to or pay attention to.

homage
(*OM-ij*)
NOUN: Display of special respect or honor; great show of reverence or allegiance.

hostile
(*HOS-tuhl*)
ADJECTIVE: Unfriendly; antagonistic.

hostility
(*ho-STIL-ih-tee*)
NOUN: Behavior that is hostile.

hunger
(*HUHN-ger*)
NOUN: A desire or craving.

> *The young prince's desire for the throne went simply beyond want—he had a HUNGER for the throne and title his older brother recently assumed.*

hunger for
(*HUHN-ger for*)
VERB: To have a strong desire for.

I

Iago

(*ee-AH-goh*)

NOUN: A character in Shakespeare's *Othello* who is consumed with jealousy.

idol

(*AHYD-l*)

NOUN: A worshiped image; a figure of a god; any personage who is the object of devotion.

idolatry

(*ahy-DOL-uh-tree*)

NOUN: The worship of a physical object as though it were a god or idol; an unusual and/or worshipful attachment to an object.

idolize

(*AHYD-l-ahyz*)

VERB: To worship or love excessively.

Watching his sons IDOLIZE their uncle and fight for his attention caused their father to feel a childlike pain as they seemingly discarded him.

ill feeling

(*ill feel-ing*)

NOUN: Resentment or animosity toward someone or something.

ill will
(*ill will*)
NOUN: Hostile or malignant feelings.

imitate
(*IM-ih-tayt*)
VERB: To mimic or follow someone else's example.

imitation
(*im-ih-TAY-shuhn*)
NOUN: The act of imitating.

imitator
(*IM-ih-tayt-or*)
NOUN: A person who mimics or follows.

immerse
(*ih-MURS*)
VERB: To completely submerge.

immoral
(*ih-MOR-uhl*)
ADJECTIVE: Not going along with established moral standards.

Love looks through a

telescope; envy,

through a microscope.

—Josh Billings

immoralism

(*ih-MOR-uhl-ism*)

NOUN: A system that does not go along with established moral standards.

impersonator

(*im-PUR-suhn-ay-ter*)

NOUN: One who imitates or mimics another person.

impression

(*im-PRESH-uhn*)

NOUN: An imitation of a person's mannerisms, voice, speech, etc.

> *While Nicholas wanted to make everyone laugh with his demeaning IMPRESSION of Kevin, everyone at the party actually felt sorry for him because his jealous intentions shone through the performance.*

indignant

(*in-DIG-nunt*)

ADJECTIVE: Marked by indignation; offended by behavior perceived as unjust or immoral; angered.

indignation

(*in-dig-NAY-shuhn*)

NOUN: Displeasure at what is perceived as unfair or unjust treatment.

indignity

(*in-DIG-ni-tee*)

NOUN: Treatment marked by losing one's dignity; shame.

infatuated

(*in-FACH-oo-ayt-ed*)

VERB: Having a passion for something or someone, often temporary or short-lived.

> *The politician's opponents went green with envy once he began speaking to the INFATUATED crowd who hung on every word he said.*

infatuation

(*in-fach-oo-AY-shun*)

NOUN: The state of being infatuated.

infirmity

(*in-FUR-mih-tee*)

NOUN: A physical ailment. Sometimes the word is used to denote a mental weakness, such as being overly cautious.

infraction

(*in-FRAK-shuhn*)

NOUN: Breaking of the rules.

insecure

(*in-si-KYOOR*)

ADJECTIVE: Lacking in self-confidence; anxious that others are judging oneself.

insecurity

(*in-si-KYOOR-ih-tee*)

NOUN: The state of being insecure; lacking in confidence.

intolerant

(*in-TOL-er-uhnt*)

ADJECTIVE: Unwilling to accept deviations from one's own opinion; unwilling to tolerate.

invidia

(*in-VI-dee-uh*)

NOUN: Spite at the successes of other people.

invidious

(*in-VID-ee-uss*)

ADJECTIVE: Likely to damage a reputation.

invidiousness

(*in-VID-ee-us-ness*)

NOUN: The state of being invidious.

irritation

(*eer-ih-TAY-shuhn*)

NOUN: State of annoyance or anger.

After weeks and weeks of unwanted attention from an overzealous ex-lover, the woman's IRRITATION grew into fury.

itch

(*itch*)

VERB: A strong desire.

J and K

jaundice
(*JAWN-diss*)
NOUN: A yellowish tint to the body's skin, fluids, and tissues as a result of the buildup of excessive bile; also, a biased, hostile attitude.

jaundiced eye
(*JAWN-dissd eye*)
NOUN: View or opinion affected by bitterness or envy.

jealous
(*JEL-us*)
ADJECTIVE: Showing or feeling envy.

jealous-type disorder
(*JEL-us-typ dis-AWR-der*)
NOUN: A psychological disorder in which someone has delusions that his or her significant other is illicitly seeing someone else.

jealousy
(*JEL-us-ee*)
NOUN: The state of being jealous.

> *It is natural to occasionally want what someone else has in passing, but allowing the feeling to fester and grow into JEALOUSY is something you should avoid.*

Envy is thin because it bites

but never eats.

—SPANISH PROVERB

jelly
(*JEL-ee*)
ADJECTIVE: A slang abbreviation for jealous.

jones
(*johnz*)
VERB: To have a craving.

just
(*just*)
ADJECTIVE: Morally fair or right.

Christina did not think it JUST that her coworkers were all invited to leave work and attend the museum's opening while she had to stay behind and take on their share of the work.

justice
(*JUST-ihs*)
NOUN: The quality of being just.

justifiable
(*just-ih-FY-uh-buhl*)
ADJECTIVE: Something done with justice.

justified
(*JUST-ih-fyd*)
ADJECTIVE: Explainable; appropriate; can be defended.

keen
(*keen*)
ADJECTIVE: Fond of; desirous.

keep up with the Joneses
(*keep uhp with thuh JOHN-sez*)
VERB: To aspire to have the same or better possessions than your neighbor.

kleptomania
(*klep-tuh-MAY-nee-uh*)
NOUN: A strong impulse or desire to steal.

L

lacking
(*LAK-ing*)

ADJECTIVE: Missing or in short supply.

> *With adventure LACKING in his current relationship,*
> *Justin wished that he could be as free as his friends*
> *who had not yet settled down.*

languish
(*LANG-wish*)

VERB: To pine for.

lascivious
(*luh-SIV-ee-us*)

ADJECTIVE: Wanton or lustful; that which excites sexual desires.

lecherous
(*LECH-er-us*)

ADJECTIVE: Excessive desire; lustful in a suggestive, potentially offensive, way.

libel
(*LYE-buhl*)

NOUN: Written defamation.

As iron is eaten by rust,

so are the envious

consumed by envy.

—Antisthenes

libelous
(*LYE-buhl-us*)
ADJECTIVE: Containing libel.

like
(*lahyk*)
VERB: To find enjoyable; to have fondness for.

lionize
(*LYE-uh-nyz*)
VERB: To praise excessively; to idolize.

long
(*lawng*)
VERB: To desire or wish.

> *The country bumpkin LONGED for a little excitement in her life and often lost herself in books in order to fill the void.*

longing
(*LAWNG-ing*)
NOUN: Yearning; a strong craving.

lust
(*luhst*)
NOUN: Strong desire.
VERB: To strongly desire or yearn for.

lustful

(*LUHST-ful*)

ADJECTIVE: Driven by lust.

lusting

(*LUHST-ing*)

VERB: To strongly desire; usually in a sexual way.

M and N

malcontent

(*MAL-kuhn-tent*)

NOUN: Someone unhappy with his or her circumstances, or with his or her government, job, lifestyle, etc.

ADJECTIVE: Unhappy with one's circumstances, government, job, lifestyle, etc.

malevolence

(*muh-LEV-uh-luhns*)

NOUN: Ill will; hatred towards others.

malevolent

(*muh-LEV-uh-lent*)

ADJECTIVE: Malicious; viciously ill-willed.

malice

(*MAL-is*)

NOUN: Desire to harm others; ill will.

malicious

(*muh-LISH-uss*)

ADJECTIVE: Spitefully mean; evil; bad intentioned.

> *The professor said his comments were all intended as constructive criticism, but I detected a MALICIOUS note in some of his suggestions.*

maliciousness

(*muh-LISH-uss-ness*)

NOUN: The quality of being malicious.

malign

(*muh-LYN*)

ADJECTIVE: Evil; malevolent.

malignity

(*muh-LIG-ni-tee*)

NOUN: An act of malice; great malice.

match

(*mach*)

NOUN: Competition.

mean-spirited

(*meen-SPEER-ih-tid*)

ADJECTIVE: Unkind; unwilling to help.

miff

(*mihf*)

NOUN: A quarrel or tiff; bad mood or huff.

miffed

(*mihfd*)

VERB: Annoyed.

Envy is the most stupid

of vices, for there is no

single advantage

to be gained from it.

—Honoré de Balzac

mistrustful

(*mis-TRUHST-ful*)

ADJECTIVE: Lacking trust.

model

(*MOD-ul*)

VERB: Follow the example of.

> *Bernard has spent his entire life wishing he were someone else, MODELING his life after those people he sees as successful and not really understanding what it is that he himself has.*

moral turpitude

(*MOR-uhl TUR-pih-tood*)

NOUN: Immoral conduct.

mortification

(*mor-tuh-fi-KAY-shuhn*)

NOUN: Humiliation or shame.

motivation

(*moh-tuh-VAY-shun*)

NOUN: The reason for doing something or behaving in a certain way; something to inspire someone to behave in a certain way.

nab

(*nab*)

VERB: To take without permission; snatch.

name-drop

(*NAYM-drop*)

VERB: To casually drop the names of famous or influential people in the course of a conversation as if to imply that one knows them on a personal level, usually as a means of self-promotion.

narcissistic personality disorder

(*NAHR-suh-siz-tik pur-suh-NAL-ih-tee dis-AWR-der*)

NOUN: A psychological condition in which someone has a preoccupation with himself or herself, as well as an inflated sense of self-importance. Envy is one of its characteristics.

need

(*need*)

NOUN: Requirement or prerequisite.

> *The line between want and NEED can run razor thin at times, especially when the need is not necessary to living but to thriving.*

needy

(*NEE-dee*)

ADJECTIVE: Demanding of attention; wanting.

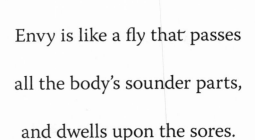

Envy is like a fly that passes

all the body's sounder parts,

and dwells upon the sores.

—Arthur Chapman

negotiate

(*ni-GOH-shee-ayt*)

VERB: To come to terms with another, typically in bargaining for goods or services, or settling on a resolution after a conflict.

neighbor

(*NAY-ber*)

NOUN: A person who lives near another; in a broader sense, fellow human beings.

nemesis

(*NEM-uh-sis*)

NOUN: An adversary or rival that one is in constant competition with.

nest egg

(*nest eg*)

NOUN: A reserve of money put aside for a specific reason; savings.

nick

(*nik*)

VERB: A British slang term meaning to steal

O

object

(*OB-jekt*)

NOUN: Any tangible or visible thing.

obloquy

(*OB-luh-kwee*)

NOUN: Public criticism; disgrace or discredit result-ing from such criticism.

> *Although he enjoyed being a civil servant, the governor*
> *ultimately stepped down, unable to bear any more*
> *OBLOQUY, instead wanting the anonymity of a*
> *civilian's life.*

obnoxious

(*uhb-NOK-shush*)

ADJECTIVE: Unpleasant; odious; annoying.

obsess

(*uhb-SESS*)

VERB: To fixate on; to be preoccupied by.

obsessive

(*uhb-SES-ihv*)

ADJECTIVE: Fixated to an extreme.

obtain

(*ub-TAYN*)

VERB: To get or acquire.

Every other sin hath some

pleasure annexed to it, or

will admit of an excuse; envy

alone wants both.

—ROBERT BURTON

odious

(*OH-dee-uhs*)

ADJECTIVE: Extremely unpleasant.

odium

(*OH-dee-um*)

NOUN: Hatred toward a person for something he or she has done.

> *The misdirected ODIUM that Ken felt was too much; he finally told the police he was not alone in the crime.*

ogle

(*OH-gul*)

VERB: To watch intently; to gaze at lasciviously.

opportunity

(*op-er-TOO-ni-tee*)

NOUN: A favorable situation, condition, or time that allows for success.

opposition

(*op-puh-ZI-shuhn*)

NOUN: Dissent, hostility.

opprobrious

(*uh-PROH-bree-us*)

ADJECTIVE: To do something with opprobrium or in a way that implies shameful conduct.

opprobrium

(uh-PROH-bree-uhm)

NOUN: Disgrace incurred by shameful conduct.

outvie

(owt-VAHY)

VERB: To outdo the competitition.

overcompensate

(oh-ver-COMP-en-sayt)

VERB: Excessively try to make amends for a perceived shortfall or weakness.

overly possessive

(OH-ver-lee puh-ZES-iv)

ADJECTIVE: Extremely possessive in nature.

P

pangs
(*pangs*)
NOUN: Sharp emotion.

Intense PANGS of jealousy coursed through Theresa's body as she watched Lisa and Mitchell, but not because she lusted after Mitchell; she simply missed being showered with affection.

pant
(*pant*)
VERB: Long for.

paranoia
(*par-uh-NOY-uh*)
NOUN: The state of being suspicious or distrustful of someone's motives; also, a mental condition characterized by delusions of persecution.

parrot
(*PAIR-et*)
VERB: To mechanically repeat or mimic.

partial
(*PAR-shul*)
ADJECTIVE: Favoring or liking someone or something, as in *partial to*.

The truest mark of being

born with great qualities is

being born without envy.

—François de La Rochefoucauld

peccability
(*pek-uh-BIL-ih-tee*)
NOUN: The state of being capable of sin or error.

peccable
(*PEK-uh-buhl*)
ADJECTIVE: Capable of sin or error.

peccadillo
(*pek-uh-DILL-oh*)
NOUN: A minor fault. *Pecadillo* comes from the Italian for "little sin."

peeved
(*peevd*)
ADJECTIVE: Annoyed.

peevishness
(*PEEV-ish-nuhs*)
NOUN: The state of being easily annoyed or irritated.

penis envy
(*PEE-nis EN-vee*)
NOUN: A woman's alleged psychological state of envy over the male's penis.

petty
(*PEH-tee*)
ADJECTIVE: A minor or small offense.

petulant
(*PET-yoo-lunt*)
ADJECTIVE: Impatiently peevish; showing great annoyance or irritation with minor problems.

pine
(*pyn*)
VERB: Desire strongly and eagerly.

pining
(*PYN-ing*)
NOUN: Yearning or longing for something or someone.

> *The couple missed the time they spent traveling together and now as parents to three children found themselves selfishly PINING for those times they could pack up and leave without a care.*

pique
(*peek*)
VERB: To engender harsh feelings by injuring a person's pride. Showing resentful irritation at a perceived slight.

possess
(*puh-ZESS*)
VERB: Own; have as a belonging.

possession
(*puh-ZESH-uhn*)
NOUN: The state of ownership. Also, an item that is owned or possessed.

possessive
(*poh-ZESS-ive*)
ADJECTIVE: Unwilling to share; desirous to own and keep things.

possessiveness
(*poh-ZESS-ihv-ness*)
NOUN: The state of being possessive.

prejudice
(*PREJ-uh-dis*)
NOUN: Bias. An opinion that is not necessarily based on fact and may have been determined beforehand.
VERB: To impose one's beliefs on someone or something; to function with a bias.

prey on
(*pray on*)
VERB: To victimize or seize.

pride
(*prayd*)
This word has several meanings, including a group
of lions and LGBTQ pride (as in a *Pride Parade*).
For the purposes of this dictionary, it means a deep
feeling of pleasure or satisfaction taken from either
one's own achievements or the achievements of
those with whom one associates.

privileged
(*PRIV-uh-lidj*)
ADJECTIVE: Having rights or advantages others do
not enjoy.

> *Even though Evan lead a much more PRIVILEGED
> life, he still envied his friend Patrick because of the
> tight bond he and his family shared.*

projection
(*proh-JEK-shuhn*)
NOUN: This word has several meanings. For the
purposes of this dictionary, it means the transfer-
ence of one's desires, fears, prejudices, etc. onto
someone else.

propinquity

(*proh-PING-kwi-tee*)

NOUN: Nearness or similarity.

provoke

(*proh-VOHK*)

VERB: To stimulate, often to the point of action.

R

rancor

(*RANG-ker*)

NOUN: Intense ill will; bitter resentment.

rancorous

(*RANG-ker-uhs*)

ADJECTIVE: Showing rancor; displaying resentment.

rankle

(*RANG-kul*)

VERB: To cause irritation or festering resentment; to be peeved by a perceived slight or oversight.

recidivism

(*rih-SID-ih-viz-um*)

NOUN: Repeated relapse into a past condition or behavior.

reciprocate

(*rih-SIP-roh-kayt*)

VERB: To give and get back in return; to experience the same emotion.

> *When she realized that her feelings towards him were not RECIPROCATED, she decided it would be best to move out of his apartment.*

relentless
(*rih-LENT-lis*)
ADJECTIVE: Unyieldingly intense or severe.

repellent
(*rih-PEL-uhnt*)
ADJECTIVE: Causing aversion or repulsion; able to repel.

repent
(*rih-PENT*)
VERB: To be sorry or repentful for transgressions.

replica
(*REP-lih-kuh*)
NOUN: A copy to scale; imitation or facsimile of an original.

replicate
(*REP-lih-kate*)
VERB: To reproduce exactly; to obtain the same results repeatedly.

repression
(*rih-PRESH-uhn*)
NOUN: The state of having suppressed thoughts or feelings.

reproduce

(*ree-proh-DOOS*)

VERB: Create something very similar to the original; obtain the same results repeatedly.

reproduction

(*ree-proh-DUK-shuhn*)

NOUN: Something that has been reproduced.

repugnance

(*rih-PUHG-nunss*)

NOUN: The state of being repugnant.

repugnant

(*rih-PUHG-nuhnt*)

ADJECTIVE: Distasteful, offensive; averse.

require

(*ree-KWYR*)

VERB: Need.

resent

(*rih-ZENT*)

VERB: To feel indignation, displeasure, or bitterness over being treated a certain way.

Hatred is active, and envy

passive dislike; there is but

one step from envy to hate.

—Johann Wolfgang von

Goethe

resentful

(*rih-ZENT-ful*)

ADJECTIVE: Feeling indignation, displeasure, or bitterness over being treated a certain way.

Bridget finally admitted to herself that she has always been somewhat RESENTFUL toward Kate since she always seems to take advantage of their friendship.

resentfulness

(*rih-ZENT-ful-nuhs*)

NOUN: The state of feeling resentful.

resentment

(*rih-ZENT-ment*)

NOUN: Indignation, displeasure, or bitterness over being treated a certain way.

retaliate

(*rih-TAL-ee-ayt*)

VERB: To get back at; to attack in a similar manner as one has been attacked.

retaliation

(*rih-tal-ee-AY-shuhn*)

NOUN: The act of getting back at.

To venture upon an

undertaking of any kind,

even the most insignificant,

is to sacrifice to envy.

—Emile M. Cioran

retaliatory

(*rih-TAL-ih-tor-ee*)

ADJECTIVE: An act denoting retaliation.

revenge

(*rih-VENJ*)

NOUN: Punishment inflicted in return for a wrong done.

revengeful

(*rih-VENJ-ful*)

ADJECTIVE: Full of revenge.

rival

(*RYV-uhl*)

NOUN: A person with whom one has a rivalry; someone competing for the same goal or goals.

rivalrous

(*RYV-uhl-russ*)

ADJECTIVE: Characterized by rivalry.

rivalry

(*RYV-uhl-ree*)

NOUN: A competition between people or teams.

True to form of any set of siblings, the two brothers had always had a strong RIVALRY, each wanting what the other had.

rivet

(RIV-it)

VERB: To hold one's attention.

S

sadness
(*SAD-nehs*)

NOUN: The state of being sad or unhappy.

> *Raymond knew that being envious would only lead to*
> *SADNESS, but he felt such a strong undeniable desire*
> *for his best friend's fiancée.*

satisfy
(*SAT-is-fy*)

VERB: To fulfill desires, expectations, or needs.

schadenfreude
(*SHAHD-n-froid*)

NOUN: A German word meaning pleasure derived from the pain of another.

seize
(*seez*)

VERB: To take hold of with force; capture or confiscate.

self-esteem
(*self-ih-STEEM*)

NOUN: Confidence in one's own worth.

settle
(*SEHT-uhl*)
VERB: Decide between several things; to come to an agreement.

shine
(*shyn*)
VERB: Take a liking to, as with *take a shine to*.

sigh for
(*sahy for*)
VERB: Desire keenly.

sin
(*sin*)
NOUN: An immoral transgression.

sinesthesia
(*sin-es-THEE-sha*)
NOUN: A slang term meaning committing all seven deadly sins—pride, envy, greed, lust, wrath, gluttony, and sloth—at once.

slander
(*SLAN-der*)
NOUN: Defamation of character.

slanderous
(*SLAN-der-us*)
ADJECTIVE: Malicious, causing defamation.

slight
(*slyt*)
VERB: To treat someone with little respect or as if he or she is of no importance.

> *Motivated simply out of her own jealous nature, Janice decided to throw a lavish party and SLIGHT the much more popular Rebecca by not inviting her to the soiree.*

smitten
(*SMIT-tuhn*)
ADJECTIVE: Very much in love; struck, as though by a hard blow.

sniveler
(*SNIV-uh-ler*)
NOUN: A person who whines or complains in a tearful way.

sore
(*soar*)
ADJECTIVE: Upset; angry.

sour
(*SOU-er*)
ADJECTIVE: Feeling of resentment or anger.

spite
(*spyt*)
NOUN: A petty desire to hurt, annoy, or humiliate someone.
VERB: To hurt, annoy, or humiliate.

spiteful
(*SPYT-ful*)
ADJECTIVE: Full of spite.

spleen
(*spleen*)
NOUN: Spite; ill temper. Origin is from the archaic belief that anger and negative feelings came from the spleen.

splenetic
(*splih-NET-ik*)
ADJECTIVE: Spiteful; bad-tempered.

spoiling for
(*SPOY-ling for*)
VERB: To behave in such a way as to invite a negative reaction; to set oneself up for.

In recompense, envy may

be the subtlest—perhaps

I should say the most

insidious—of the seven

deadly sins.

—Joseph Epstein

stalk
(*stahlk*)
VERB: To approach in a stealthy way; to obsessively pour unwanted attention on someone.

stalker
(*stahl-KER*)
NOUN: One who *stalks*.

> *With a strange infatuation and want for her lifestyle, the STALKER followed the young socialite from party to party, wishing she could be her.*

status
(*STAH-tuss*)
NOUN: One's ranking or position relative to others; the standing of a person or thing, such as social status or the status of a project.

stint
(*stint*)
VERB: To be frugal or economical about something.

sulk
(*suhlk*)
VERB: To be annoyed or disappointed, in a silent, morose way.

sullen
(*SUHL-uhn*)
ADJECTIVE: Gloomy and sulky; bad-tempered.

superior
(*suh-PEER-ee-er*)
ADJECTIVE: More accomplished or of better quality; higher in position, rank, or status.

The pair's SUPERIOR accommodations became the envy of everyone with whom they were traveling.

surly
(*SUHR-lee*)
ADJECTIVE: Unfriendly; brusque.

suspect
(*suhs-PEKT*)
VERB: To have a belief of feeling without proof.

suspicion
(*suh-SPISH-uhn*)
NOUN: A feeling or belief one has without proof.

suspicious
(*suh-SPISH-uhs*)
ADJECTIVE: The state of feeling suspicion.

suspire
(*suh-SPYR*)
VERB: To breathe in a longing, sighing manner.

sweet
(*sweet*)
ADJECTIVE: As in *sweet on;* to love someone or something.

T

take

(*tayk*)

VERB: To bring into one's possession, sometimes without permission.

take to

(*tayk to*)

VERB: To start to like something; to feel an affinity for.

talent

(*TAL-uhnt*)

NOUN: A natural ability or aptitude that sets one apart from others.

tantalize

(*TAN-tuhl-ahyz*)

VERB: To excite another by keeping a desirable object or person just out of reach.

target

(*TAHR-git*)

NOUN: A goal or objective.

tease

(*teez*)

VERB: To arouse desire without allowing that which is desired to be obtained.

Our envy always lasts longer

than the happiness of those

we envy.

—HERACLITUS EPHESUS

tempt

(*tempt*)

VERB: To attract or entice, usually to do something immoral.

temptation

(*temp-TAY-shuhn*)

NOUN: Something that attracts or entices.

the grumbles

(*thuh GRUM-bles*)

NOUN: An expression of discontent.

thirst

(*thurst*)

NOUN: The state of needing liquid; also, a strong desire or craving.

> *It only took a few moments standing in the spotlight for the young starlet to THIRST for the type of constant attention that ultimately caused her downfall.*

tiff

(*tif*)

NOUN: A brief argument or dispute.

titleholder
(*TY-tuhl-hohl-der*)
NOUN: Any person who holds a title; typically refers to a champion.

top
(*top*)
ADJECTIVE: Characterized as being the best.

toxic friend
(*TAHK-zik frend*)
NOUN: A friend who is poisonous due to jealousy issues.

transgress
(*trans-GRESS*)
VERB: To violate a principle or moral law.

transgression
(*trans-GRESH-un*)
NOUN: A violation of a rule. To break a law or guideline is to commit a *transgression*.

trespass

(*TREHS-pass*)

VERB: To enter without permission. Also, to commit an offense.

> *Breaking into Gerard's home was the ultimate*
> *TRESPASS for Michael, not because he entered*
> *unlawfully, but because he used the key Gerard*
> *entrusted him with.*

trust

(*truhst*)

NOUN: Belief or confidence placed in someone or something.

VERB: To be confident of or believe in; the act of being confident or believing in someone or something.

typify

(*TIP-uh-fy*)

VERB: To exemplify.

U and V

ulterior
(*uhl-TEER-ee-er*)
ADJECTIVE: Intentionally hidden.

umbrage
(*UM-brij*)
NOUN: As in to *take umbrage;* resentful annoyance or irritation.

umbrageous
(*uhm-BRAY-juhs*)
ADJECTIVE: Characterized by umbrage.

unabashed
(*un-uh-BASHT*)
ADJECTIVE: Not disguised; obvious.

undesirable
(*uhn-dih-ZYR-uh-buhl*)
ADJECTIVE: Unpleasant; not desirable.

unhappiness
(*un-HAP-ee-ness*)
NOUN: The state of being sad.

unhappy
(*un-HAP-ee*)
ADJECTIVE: Sad; without happiness.

unremitting
(*un-ruh-MITT-ing*)
ADJECTIVE: Persistent; relentless.

> *The UNREMITTING pain Walter felt because of Alice's absence in his life was made that much worse when he realized she had moved on to another man.*

unrest
(*un-REST*)
NOUN: A state of discontent; dissatisfaction.

unvirtuous
(*un-VUR-choo-uhs*)
ADJECTIVE: Not conforming to moral principles.

upstage
(*UHP-stayj*)
VERB: To outdo or overshadow.

urge
(*uhrj*)
NOUN: An impulse or strong desire.

Probably the greatest harm done by vast wealth is the harm that we of moderate means do ourselves when we let the vices of envy and hatred enter deep into our own natures.

—Theodore Roosevelt

valuable

(*VAL-yoo-uh-buhl*)

ADJECTIVE: Having great monetary worth.
NOUN: Any object with great worth, usually
referred to in the plural.

venial sin

(*VEE-nee-uhl sin*)

NOUN: A sin that is slight or minor, as contrasted
with *mortal sin*.

vicarious

(*viy-KAYR-ee-uss*)

ADJECTIVE: Arising from the experiences of others
rather than oneself, as in *vicarious pleasure*.

vie

(*vahy*)

VERB: To compete with.

> *Both of the young children always want to be the center
> of attention and will VIE for their parents' notice
> whenever they are in the same room.*

vigilant

(*VIJ-uh-lunt*)

ADJECTIVE: Alert; watchful of danger.

virulence
(*VIR-yuh-lens*)
NOUN: Bitter hostility.

virulent
(*VIR-yuh-lent*)
ADJECTIVE: Poisonous or intensely hostile. *Virulent* shares the same root as *virus*.

vitriolic
(*vit-ree-OL-ik*)
ADJECTIVE: Acidic, literally or in tone; harsh, caustic.

vying
(*VAHY-ing*)
ADJECTIVE: The act of competing.

W and X

waiting list
(*WAY-ting list*)
NOUN: A list of people waiting, as for reservations, appointments, or to fill a vacancy when open.

want
(*wahnt*)
VERB: Desire; wish; crave.

> *The WANT of jealousy does not go away even if the possession is obtained; it only sets its sights on some other target.*

wanting
(*WAHTN-ing*)
ADJECTIVE: Desirous. Also, lacking or in need of.

ware
(*wayr*)
NOUN: Merchandise or goods, usually referred to in the plural.

wariness
(*WAYR-ee-nis*)
NOUN: The quality or state of being wary.

The wicked envy and hate;

it is their way of admiring.

—Victor Hugo

wary
(*WAYR-ee*)
ADJECTIVE: On guard; watchful of danger; leery; suspicious.

watchful
(*WACH-ful*)
ADJECTIVE: Vigilant; observing closely.

wealth
(*WELTH*)
NOUN: An abundance of some quality or possession, such as money, property, or love.

wicked
(*WIK-id*)
ADJECTIVE: Evil; sinful.

wish
(*wish*)
VERB: To long for; desire; want.
NOUN: A fervent longing or desire.

> *Every year on her birthday, Margot would WISH to be as beautiful as her sister Elizabeth—little did she know that Elizabeth wished to be as smart as Margot.*

wishful
(*WISH-ful*)
ADJECTIVE: Having or expressing a longing for something or someone.

womb envy
(*woom EN-vee*)
NOUN: A man's alleged psychological state of jealousy over a woman having a womb. The opposite of penis envy.

wronged
(*rawngd*)
ADJECTIVE: Incorrect or unfair treatment.

Y and Z

⤬

yank
(*yangk*)
VERB: To grab or snatch abruptly.

yearn
(*yurn*)
VERB: To pine or long for intensely.

> *It took him years to realize what a fool he was to leave such a wonderful woman, and when he did he was left YEARNING for her as she went on to marry another man.*

yearning
(*YUR-ning*)
NOUN: Strong desire or longing.

yen
(*yen*)
NOUN: A desire, craving, or longing.

There is not a passion so

strongly rooted in the human

heart as envy.

—RICHARD BRINSLEY SHERIDAN

zeal

(*zeel*)

NOUN: Fervor and enthusiasm; ardor.

zero in

(*ZEE-ro ihn*)

VERB: To set one's sights on.

Envy feeds on the living.

It ceases when they are dead.

—OVID

DAILY BENDER

Want Some More?

Hit up our humor blog, The Daily Bender, to get your fill of all things funny—be it subversive, odd, offbeat, or just plain mean. The Bender editors are there to get you through the day and on your way to happy hour. Whether we're linking to the latest video that made us laugh or calling out (or bullshit on) whatever's happening, we've got what you need for a good laugh.

If you like our book, you'll love our blog. (And if you hated it, "man up" and tell us why.) Visit The Daily Bender for a shot of humor that'll serve you until the bartender can.

Sign up for our newsletter at
www.adamsmedia.com/blog/humor
and download our Top Ten Maxims No Man Should Live Without.